MICHIGAN GOVERNORS GROWING UP

by

Willah Weddon

First Edition
Published by NOG Press
325B North Clippert Street
Lansing, MI 48912

ISBN 0-9638376-1-3

Library of Congress Catalog Number: 93-94953

Illustrations: Kathi Terry

CONTENTS

INTRODUCTION

The Governor is the head of Michigan's government. He has the State Legislators to help him. They are called Senators and Representatives. All of them are elected by the people. They work in the State Capitol building in Lansing.

We have had 44 governors since Michigan became a state in 1837. Many of them were poor when they were young. They had to work hard to get an education.

Four governors were not yet 12 years old when both their mother and father died. They were orphans. Who raised them?

The mother or father of four other governors died before they were 10 years old. How did they grow up?

Many governors came from large families. There were 16 children in Governor Moses Wisner's family. Did you know that Governor John Engler has six brothers and sisters?

As you read about these governors, you will learn how they grew into good men. They worked to make Michigan a great state for us to live in today.

GOVERNOR STEVENS T. MASON
1835 THROUGH 1839

Stevens Thomson Mason was a pretty baby. He was the only boy in the family. He had six sisters. They called him "Tom" and they adored him.

Stevens was born in Virginia, on October 27, 1811. Then the family moved to Lexington, Kentucky. He was raised there.

Stevens' father was John T. Mason. He was a lawyer and businessman. Stevens studied at the University of Transylvania. But hard times hit. Stevens' father lost his fortune. Stevens had to leave school. He took a job as a grocer's clerk.

President Andrew Jackson gave Stevens' father a job. He was named Secretary of Michigan Territory in 1830. The family moved to Detroit.

2

Stevens was 18 years old. He spent a lot of time helping his father in office. When his father was gone, Stevens tended to the office. He learned all about it.

Then his father decided to go to Texas in 1831. President Jackson named Stevens to take his father's job as territorial secretary. Some people didn't like this idea. They thought he was too young. They told Stevens to give up the job. He told them, politely, to mind their own business. They decided to give him a chance.

When the Territorial Governors went on trips, Stevens filled in for them. He did a good job. The people changed their minds. They liked young Stevens Mason.

While he was working he also studied law and became a lawyer. He dreamed that Michigan would become a state.

He sent troops to help when Indians in Illinois caused trouble. He sent troops to keep the Toledo Strip in Michigan Territory. President Jackson called him a "Young Hotspur." He sent another secretary to the territory.

But Stevens got the people to vote to make Michigan a state. They elected him governor. A year later Congress voted to let Michigan become a state. Now Mason was really the governor. He was 24 years old.

The Ann Arbor paper called him the "Boy Governor." Mason didn't like this. He caught the reporter that wrote the story and thrashed him.

Stevens and his younger sister, Emily, were good friends. They rode their horses along the streets of Detroit. The streets were dirt roads then.

There were many things a new state needed. Stevens had ideas for schools, prisons, roads and canals.

He was re-elected governor. The legislature told him to go to New York to borrow money they needed. He met Julia Phelps while he was there. He went back later and married her. She came to Detroit but it was too wild for her. She went home to New York.

The money Stevens had borrowed didn't come through. A depression hit the country and the state was in debt. Stevens got the blame. When his term was up as governor, he went to New York, too.

Three years later Stevens Mason died on January 4, 1843. He was only 31 years old. Sixty years later his body was brought back to Detroit. There is a statue of him today in downtown Detroit.

GOVERNOR WILLIAM WOODBRIDGE
1840 AND 1841

Life was serious business for William Woodbridge. He was always fighting for something.

William was the second son of Dudley and Lucy Woodbridge. He was born on August 20, 1780, in Connecticut.

When he was about nine years old, his mother and father moved to Marietta, Ohio. William and his brother were left behind. They stayed with a cousin so they could go to school. It was two years before their father brought them to Ohio in a wagon.

Marietta was on the frontier. There was danger from the Indians on the warpath. William went to the school in the town block house. He learned some grammar and the multiplication tables.

He spent a year in a French village, Gallipolis, and learned to speak French. He also worked in a law office in Marietta. He became a good friend of Lewis Cass, who was later appointed Territorial Governor of Michigan.

When he was 16, William was sent back to Connecticut. He studied at the famous law school at Litchfield. He met Juliana Trumbull here. She was beautiful. He fell in love.

Woodbridge finished law school and returned to Marietta. He and Juliana wrote to each other for two years. Then he went to Connecticut to marry her. They came back to Ohio. He was soon into politics. He was in the Ohio senate until 1815.

His old friend Governor Lewis Cass then asked Woodbridge to come and be Secretary of the Territory. Woodbridge said he would do it. He spent two weeks going through the Black Swamp to get to Detroit. It was January 1815, when he got there.

Things weren't very good in Detroit. The Indians were causing trouble. Cass was gone often on trips. Woodbridge had to do his job as well as his own.

He felt better when Juliana came to Detroit a year later. She brought their baby girl with her. He had bought some land along the river. They had a house there. They had five more children, but two of them died.

Woodbridge was sent to Washington as a representative from the territory. He didn't get paid for a long time. He worried about money. He worried about Juliana and the children back in Detroit. He came home and didn't go back until years later.

President John Quincy Adams appointed him to the Territorial Supreme Count. After four years he was elected to the Michigan Senate. He didn't like the things Governor Stevens T. Mason was doing. They didn't like each other.

He said Mason had been elected illegally. He said Mason had put the state into debt. Mason was a Democrat. Woodbridge was a Whig. He ran for governor and he won the election. He was the only Whig ever elected Governor of Michigan.

Woodbridge was in office only a year when he was elected to the U.S. Senate. His Lieutenant Governor, James Wright Gordon, became Governor. Woodbridge went to Washington again. This time he stayed for six years.

When he came back to Michigan, Detroit was growing fast. The city was taking over his farm. He had to fight to keep it until he died on October 20, 1861. He was 81 years old. Today Tiger Stadium stands on a part of the Woodbridge farm.

5

GOVERNOR JAMES WRIGHT GORDON
1841

Not much is known about James Gordon's childhood. But strange things happened in his life. He had a throat problem and his voice was husky. But he learned to be a good speaker. He got to be governor because some Senators tricked him. He died mysteriously. No one knows where he is buried.

He was born at Plainfield, Connecticut in 1809. His father had served in the Army and was a politician.

He had a brother, Alexander.

When James was young, his family moved to Geneva, New York. He went to school there. He left for college then came back and taught school at Geneva. While there, he studied law and became a lawyer.

At Geneva he met Mary Hudun and they were married. They moved to Marshall, Michigan in 1835. They had five children. (His oldest son grew up to be a lawyer, too.)

Gordon had a law office in Marshall. He wanted Marshall to be the capital of Michigan. Some friends told him Marshall would be the new capital when it was moved from Detroit. He built a house and it was called the Governor's Mansion. It was built on a small hill he called Capitol Hill. He was a member of the Whig party and very popular. He was a Michigan Senator for a year and then he was elected Lieutenant Governor of Michigan.

He thought his friends in the Senate would elect him to the U.S. Senate in Washington. He went to a dinner to celebrate. But while he was celebrating, some of his Whig friends joined up with the Democrats. The next morning they elected Governor William Woodbridge to the U.S. Senate. The politicians laughed over this trick for a long time.

When Governor Woodbridge left for Washington, Gordon became Governor of Michigan. And for the next ten months his house in Marshall was the Governor's Mansion. It wasn't until six years later that the capital was moved from Detroit to Lansing. Marshall didn't get to be the capital after all.

Gordon went back to Marshall when his time as governor ended. He still wanted to be a Senator in Washington. Five years later he tried again, but he never got elected to the Senate.

He was still having trouble with his throat and lungs. President Zachary Taylor asked him to go to South America as a consul for the government. Gordon thought it would help his health, so in 1849 he and Mary went to Brazil.

About three years after he got there, he died from an accident. He had a coughing fit and fell off a balcony at the consulate. He was 44 years old. Mary returned to New York. No one has ever found out where he was buried.

GOVERNOR JOHN S. BARRY
1842 THROUGH 1845, 1850 AND 1851

John Steward Barry was born in New Hampshire, on January 29, 1802. His parents moved to a farm in Vermont when he was young. He had two brothers, Charles and Aldis. He worked on his father's farm and went to the country school. He studied by himself until he was 21. Then he went on his own.

John married Mary Kidder in Vermont and they moved to Georgia. He taught school for two years and studied law. He became captain of a company of State militia and became a Governor's Aide.

John and Mary left Georgia in 1831 and moved to White Pigeon, Michigan. He started a dry goods store. In three years they moved to Constantine. The St. Joseph River ran through the town. He owned boats and they brought supplies for his store. He was very successful.

He liked to talk politics with people in the store. He knew the laws and they soon elected him to offices. They elected him to go to the Territorial Legislature. They picked him to go to the convention and help make up a Constitution for Michigan. Then, when Michigan was a state, they elected him to the Michigan Senate. He was a Democrat.

Barry became well known. He was elected Governor of Michigan two times. He wasn't a very good speaker and he was awkward. But he was sensible. The Detroit Free Press said he was "an honest man." He was careful with his own money. He was careful with the state's money.

When he ran for re-election, he was called "Blue Ruin" by some enemies. But the people wanted him to be governor and elected him.

After two terms in office, Barry left for home. At that time the constitution said a man could be governor only two times in a row.

When he got back to Constantine, Barry tended to his business. He and Mary built a big, new house. But the people didn't forget him.

Governor Alpheus Felch had been elected but left for the U.S. Senate. His Lieutenant Governor, William Greenly, finished the term for him. Governor Epaphroditus Ransom was elected next. He would have run a second time but the Democrats didn't want him.

The Democrats had a meeting and picked Barry to run again. He wasn't at their meeting. When he heard about it, Barry said he would run. He did and he won the election.

By this time the capital had been moved from Detroit to Lansing. So Barry went to Lansing. Mary visited the town a few times but she liked home best.

A new constitution was written during these two years. Then Barry went back again to Constantine.

Barry ran two more times, later on, for governor. But he didn't win.

He died at his home in Constantine when he was 67 years old.

The house the Barrys lived in is now a museum in Constantine.

GOVERNOR ALPHEUS FELCH
1846 AND 1847

Alpheus Felch was such a sickly baby that he wasn't expected to live very long. He survived, but he had a hard life when he was young.

Alpheus was the only boy in the family. He had five sisters. He was born on September 28, 1804, in Limerick, Maine. His father was a merchant.

His father died when he was two years old. His mother died when he was little more than three years old.

10

His sisters were sent to live with relatives. Alpheus was sent to live with his grandfather, Abijah Felch. But six years later Abijah died. Alpheus went to live with his other grandfather and an aunt.

But the orphan boy got a good education. He went to college and became a lawyer. Then his doctor told him he must move to a warmer climate or he would die.

Alpheus started for Mississippi, but he met a girl in Monroe, Michigan. Her name was Lucretia. He decided to stay in Monroe and marry her. They had eight children.

He got into politics. He was elected a State Representative. He was named to state offices and became a justice on the Supreme Court.

He was elected Governor of Michigan. Before his two years were up, he was elected to the U.S. Senate in Washington. He was there for six years.

Alpheus returned to his home in Ann Arbor. He became a professor in the law school at the University of Michigan.

He was a kind man. He never swore. He never got angry at people.

They didn't think he'd live when he was a baby. But Alpheus Felch lived longer than any other Michigan Governor. He was 91 years old when he died in 1896.

GOVERNOR WILLIAM L. GREENLY
1847

When Governor Alpheus Felch was elected a U.S. Senator, he left for Washington. His Lieutenant Governor, William Greenly, became Governor of Michigan. He was Governor for ten months.

Greenly was the son of Thomas and Nancy Greenly. He was born in New York on September 18, 1813. He graduated from college at the age of 19. Then he studied and became a lawyer.

Greenly was married to a girl named Sarah Dascomb from Hamilton, New York. She must have died. But there are no records. He moved to Adrian, Michigan.

He opened a law office in Adrian. A few years later he was elected to the Michigan Senate. He went back east and married another girl, Elizabeth Hubbard. He was elected to another term in the Michigan Senate.

Then Greenly was elected Lieutenant Governor. Little more than a year after this, Governor Felch left for Washington. Greenly was now the governor.

He signed the bill to move the state capital from Detroit to Lansing. He also sent Michigan troops to the Mexican war.

When his term was over, Greenly went back to Adrian. He was elected mayor of Adrian. A year later, Elizabeth died. They had two sons.

About nine years later (1859), Greenly married Maria Hart from Adrian. He died at the age of 70, in 1883.

GOVERNOR EPAPHRODITUS RANSOM
1848 AND 1849

How would you like to have a name like Epaphroditus? It wasn't odd when Epaphroditus Ransom was a boy. But when he was older he signed some papers, "Epaphro". Maybe he didn't like the name too much himself.

Epaphroditus was born in Massachusetts, on March 24, 1798. He was the oldest son. He had 11 brothers and sisters. They moved to Vermont when he was young.

He worked on the family farm and he went to the country school. Then he studied law and became a lawyer.

Epaphro Ransom was tall and had dark hair. He opened an office in Townshend, Vermont. He was elected to the legislature in Montpelier. Here he met Almira Cadwell and they were married in 1827.

Two of his brothers and a sister moved to Michigan. They wrote and told him it was a great place to live. He packed up his wife and their two children. They came by boat on the river and by wagon over land. It took them a month to get to Bronson, Michigan. The village was called Kalamazoo, later on.

They lived in a log cabin the first winter. Wolves howled at their door. In the spring Ransom built a law office and a house next to it.

Governor Mason appointed Ransom to be a Circuit Court Judge. He rode his horse all over western Michigan to hold court. He was appointed to the Supreme Court. In 1843 Governor Barry appointed him the Chief Justice of the Supreme Court. He liked being a judge.

Kalamazoo was growing fast. Ransoms had their house moved out to a large farm site. They raised sheep and cattle. They had big orchards.

The Democrats wanted him to run for governor. He was elected. The new State House had been built now in Lansing. Ransom was the first governor to take office there.

He got the state to build plank roads. They were built by laying planks of wood on the ground. People had to pay to drive their horses and wagons on them. When the wood rotted, the horses could stumble.

But Ransom thought logs were just the thing for roads.

The Democrats didn't let him run a second time for governor. They picked John Barry who had been governor before. But Ransom was elected to the Michigan Legislature for one term. Then he went into the banking business and the plank road business with his son. He lost all his money. He wasn't well. He was very discouraged.

Then President James Buchanan appointed him to an office in Kansas. He and Almira moved to Fort Scott. He sold government land to settlers. Ransom died there after about two years, on November 11, 1859. His body was brought back to Michigan and he was buried in Kalamazoo.

GOVERNOR ROBERT MCCLELLAND
1851 UNTIL MARCH 8, 1853

Governor Robert McClelland always looked very serious. But he loved to laugh. He liked to hear funny things.

Robert was born at Greencastle, Pennsylvania on August 1, 1807. His father was a doctor. He went to good schools. But when he was 17 years old, he was on his own.

He taught school to earn money to go to college. He graduated first in his class. Then he taught school again to pay his way through law school.

McClelland had a law office in Pittsburgh for a year. Then he headed west. He settled in Monroe, Michigan. He liked politics. He was at the 1835 convention that wrote a constitution for Michigan. This was before Michigan was a state.

In 1837 he married Elizabeth Sarah Sabin from Massachusetts. They had six children.

He was elected to the Michigan Legislature in 1838. Then he was elected three times to go to Washington as a U.S. Senator.

When he returned to Michigan, he was at the 1850 convention to write a new constitution for the state. The next year he ran for governor on the Democrat's ticket. He won the election and was Governor for a year.

The new constitution said the Governor could only serve one year. Then he could be elected for a two-year term. This is what he did.

But very soon after he was re-elected, he left for Washington. President Franklin Pierce named him Secretary of the Interior. His Lieutenant Governor, Andrew Parsons, became Governor.

After four years in Washington, McClelland came back to Detroit. He was a delegate to the 1867 convention to write another constitution. He is the only governor who went to three of these conventions.

McClelland died on August 30, 1880. He was 73 years old. He was buried in Detroit.

GOVERNOR ANDREW PARSONS
1853 AND 1854

Andrew Parsons was a New Yorker. Both his parents had come to America from Ireland. The Parsons were as Irish as they could be.

Not much is known about his childhood. Andrew was born in Hoosick, New York on July 22, 1817. He had at least two brothers, Luke and Titus. When he was 17, he came to Michigan. He probably made the long trip with his brothers. They lived in Michigan, too. They were both lawyers and in politics.

After they got to Michigan, Parsons taught school in Ann Arbor for a while. He finally settled in Shiawassee County. He studied law and he was the county prosecuting attorney.

He married Elvira Howe and they had two children, Daniel and Esther.

Parsons was elected to the Michigan Senate for a term. Then he returned to the village of Corunna, where they lived in Shiawassee County.

Elvira died and he married Anna Marilla Ferrand Stewart. She was a widow with three children. He and Anna Marilla had two children, Elvina and Andrew. That made seven children in the family.

Parsons was chosen to be a Regent of the University of Michigan. Then he was elected Lieutenant Governor on the Democrat's ticket.

He took office in January 1853. But in March, Governor McClelland left for Washington. The President had appointed McClelland to run the Department of Interior.

This meant that Lieutenant Governor Parsons became Governor. He was Governor for nearly the full two-year term. He was a good speaker. He was a firm and reliable governor.

The railroads tried to tell him what to do. He wouldn't call a special session of the legislature. They didn't like it. But they respected him.

While he was Governor an important meeting was held in Jackson. Whigs and Democrats and others joined together. They were against slavery. They drew up papers saying, "We will....be known as Republicans."

The Republicans picked Kinsley S. Bingham to run for Governor.

The Democrats were afraid Parsons would lose the election. So they asked former Governor Barry to run instead. Barry agreed to run, but he lost.

Since he was not running for governor, Parsons ran for the legislature. He was elected. He was not well, though. He went back to Corunna. His baby son, Andrew, was born soon after he got back. In a few months, Parsons died on June 6, 1855. He was only 37 years old.

GOVERNOR KINSLEY S. BINGHAM
1855 THROUGH 1858

The first Republican Governor of Michigan was Kinsley Bingham.

He was born in 1808, in Camillus, New York. His father's name was Calvin and his mother's name was Betsey. He had a younger bother, Henry, and a sister named Caroline. They all worked on their family farm.

Kinsley went to school and then studied in a law office to be a lawyer.

Two girls came to Camillus and this changed Kinsley's life. They were Margaret and Janet Warden from Scotland. Their brother, Robert Warden, came later when he was 17 years old. He came on a sailing vessel and was 45 days on the voyage.

Kinsley and Margaret got married. Then, with Janet and Robert, they drove by horse and wagon to Michigan. They bought 400-acres of land in Green Oak Township, Livingston County.

They began clearing the land and built a double log house. Margaret had a baby boy, Kinsley Warden, and she died four days later. Janet took care of the baby.

Bingham soon took part in politics. He was a Justice of the Peace, then Postmaster, then Judge of Probate in the county. Next he was elected to the Michigan Legislature in 1837. He was re-elected four times.

No one stayed in the state capital very long in those days. They did their business in two or three months and went back home. Bingham came back to the farm where things were happening.

Mr. and Mrs. Warden came from Scotland to live on the farm. They brought their youngest daughter, Mary, with them. Bingham and Mary got married. They had a little boy, James. They built a beautiful house near Green Oak.

Bingham's sister, Caroline, married Robert Warden and came to live at Green Oak. Bingham's brother, Henry, moved to Grass Lake and owned a store there.

For four years, Bingham was a Congressman in Washington. Mary went with him some of the time. He had always been a Democrat. But he was against slavery and joined the Free Soil party.

When the Whigs and some Democrats met in Jackson in 1854, Bingham joined

them. He got the other Free Soilers to join, too. They formed the Republican party. They nominated Bingham for governor. He won the election.

Bingham worked for laws that would help the slaves who escaped to Michigan. He was re-elected for two more years. He was called the farmer governor. He got the State Agricultural College in operation. (It is now Michigan State University.)

After he was governor for two terms, he was elected to the U.S. Senate. He went to Washington again. He took Mary to Abraham Lincoln's Inaugural Ball in Washington.

But Bingham was in the Senate for less than two years. He was home on their farm when he died suddenly on October 5, 1861. The Bingham house is still standing near South Lyon. Part of it is the Green Oak Historical Society.

GOVERNOR MOSES WISNER
1859 AND 1860

There were 16 children in Moses Wisner's family. He was the 12th. He was born on June 2, 1815 in Springport, New York. They all worked on their parent's farm.

One of his older brothers, George, came to Pontiac, Michigan, in 1835. George studied law and set up a law office there.

Two years later Michigan became a state. Moses was 22 years old. He came to Michigan, too. He bought land in Lapeer County. For two years he chopped down trees. He planted small fields. He decided he wasn't getting ahead. So he jumped on his horse and rode to Pontiac. He studied law with his brother.

When he became a lawyer, Moses went back to Lapeer. He opened an office. He married Eliza Richardson from New York. They had a son, Edward, born in 1842.

Two years later, Moses moved back to Pontiac. He joined his brother's law firm. He did well. He bought a farm. Then his wife died. He had little Edward to raise.

Moses Wisner was well built. He had black hair. When he spoke to people, they believed him. When he decided to do something, he did it. Four years went by until he met Angeolina Hascall from Flint. He was 33. She was 20. She wasn't sure she wanted to get married. He was sure he did. They had a wedding in 1838.

Their home was called Pine Grove. He bought more land all the time. They had three children.

Wisner and his brother were both Whigs. But Moses went to the meeting in Jackson and became a Republican. He ran for Congress and lost. He ran for a U.S. Senate seat and lost.

Then he ran for Governor and he won. It was his first and only political victory. He went to Lansing but Angeolina stayed home. They entertained people in their house.

He did not run for a second term as governor. The State Treasurer had taken the state's money. It wasn't Wisner's fault, but he felt bad about it.

The Civil War broke out right after he returned to Pontiac. The new governor, Austin Blair, appointed Wisner to organize an Infantry Regiment.

Wisner became a Colonel. He trained 997 men in a camp near his house. Then they left for Kentucky to fight in the war.

The winter of 1862 was a cold one. Many soldiers were sick. Wisner got sick, too. His son, Edward, was in his regiment. Edward and Angeolina were with Wisner when he died on January 5, 1863. His body was brought back to Pontiac and he was buried there.

The Wisner house in Pontiac is a museum today.

GOVERNOR AUSTIN BLAIR
1861 THROUGH 1864

Austin Blair is known as Michigan's War Governor. He was governor only a few months when the Civil War started. He was governor for four years. By then the Civil War was nearly over.

His father felled the first tree in Tompkins County, New York. He burned the first log heap. He built the first log cabin there. And this is where Austin Blair was born on February 8, 1818.

Both his mother, Rhoda Blackman, and his father, George, were strong against slavery. Austin had strong opinions, too. Sometimes they got him into trouble.

He began studying Latin when he was 16 years old. He went to a college and protested against a rule. He went to Union college and fought against secret societies. He was an independent thinker.

He studied law and became a lawyer. Then he came to Jackson, Michigan, to practice law. He married Persis Lyman and they moved to Eaton County. They had a baby girl, but both Persis and the baby died. He was heart-broken. He moved back to Jackson.

Blair opened a law office in Jackson. He was elected to the Michigan Legislature in 1846. He got married again. He married Elizabeth Pratt. They had a baby boy and both Elizabeth and the baby died.

Two years later he married a widow, Sarah Ford. They had four sons and one daughter. They built a big house in Jackson. Blair was Jackson County Prosecutor. He was a Whig.

When the Republican party was formed in Jackson, Blair became a Republican. He was in the Michigan Senate for two years. Then he was elected Governor of Michigan.

Three months after he took office, the Civil War began. President Lincoln needed troops. There wasn't any money left in the state treasury. The State Treasurer had taken it. So Blair raised money himself and sent soldiers to help. Word came not to train any more soldiers. Blair ignored the message. It wasn't long before the President called for more men. Michigan was ready, thanks to Governor Blair.

Michigan sent more than 90,000 men to war before peace was declared. Blair was considered one of the best war governors in all

the United States. But he used a lot of his own money. He left Lansing and returned to Jackson a poor man.

He was elected to Congress in 1867 and re-elected two times. While in Washington he still spoke his mind. He left the Republican party. He came back to Jackson and ran again for governor. He didn't win.

By now he had a big family. His sons had married and had children. He had a parrot named Loretta. When he came into his library, Loretta would say, "Hello Grandpa," over and over until he'd say, "Hello Loretta, now be quiet."

He wanted to be a U.S. Senator, but he was never elected. He was named to the Board of Regents of the University of Michigan. He wasn't well. His son helped him in his law office in Jackson. They didn't have much business.

Blair died on August 6, 1894 and was buried in Mount Evergreen Cemetery. A year later plans were made for a statue of him. His statue is standing today on the lawn of the Capitol building in Lansing.

GOVERNOR HENRY H. CRAPO
1865 THROUGH 1868

Things didn't come easy for Henry Howland Crapo when he was a boy. He was born on May 24, 1804, at Dartmouth, Massachusetts. He was the eldest son in the family. He had two brothers, David and Joseph, and a sister, Phebe. They lived on a farm with very poor soil. They barely made a living.

Henry decided he didn't want to be poor all his life. He knew he would have to get an education. So he began studying when he was a boy. He made a list of words he heard. Then he walked seven miles to a library to look them up in a dictionary. He wrote the meanings down. He made his own dictionary.

Later, he found a book about surveying. He studied it and wanted to get a job surveying. He needed a compass to do the work. He didn't have money to buy one. So he went to a Blacksmith's shop and made one. He got the job.

He became a village teacher, too. Then he studied some more. He walked 15 miles to take a test for a job in a high school. He passed the test and got the job.

He was teaching when he married Mary Ann Slocum. Her people were Friends, as the English Quakers were called. Her father was rich and he didn't want her to marry Henry. Henry was not a Friend. Henry didn't own any property. He didn't make much money teaching school.

But her father finally agreed. Henry and Mary Ann were married. She lived with her parents for several years. They had two children while she was there. Henry walked 20 miles on Saturdays to see her. He walked 20 miles back on Sundays to teach school the next week. Henry was a walker.

They saved money this way. Henry bought real estate and did other jobs to earn money. At last, in 1828, they had a home of their own in New Bedford, Massachusetts. He was a Colonel in the State militia. By 1856 they had ten children. One boy and nine girls. They were wealthy.

Over the years Henry Crapo had bought a lot of land in Michigan. It was covered with pine trees. He decided they should move to Flint to take care of the property. It was hard to leave their beautiful home.

But Crapo soon had five lumber mills going at one time. He started the Flint and Holly Railroad. He bought a 1,385-acre farm in Swartz Creek. He was a lumber baron.

He was also interested in seeing Flint grow. He was mayor of the city. Then he was elected a State Senator. He was a Whig, but joined the Republican party when it was formed.

He was elected governor in 1865 on the Republican ticket and re-elected two years later. While he was Governor he wouldn't sign bills giving aid to the railroads. He wanted the state to "pay as we go," and stay out of debt.

Although he was sick some of the time, Crapo worked very hard in Lansing. When his term was up in January, he went back to Flint. He died seven months later on July 22, 1869. His grandson, Billy Durant, started General Motors Corporation in Flint.

GOVERNOR HENRY P. BALDWIN
1869 THROUGH 1872

There were 15 children in the Baldwin family. Henry was the 12th child. He was born in Rhode Island on February 22, 1814.

Both his parents died by the time he was 11 years old. Henry had to go to work. He was clerk in a store at the age of 12. For the next six years he studied when he wasn't working in the store. Then he opened his own business. He married Harriet Day in 1835.

Henry and Harriet came to Detroit in the spring of 1838. He started a shoe and boot business. He became a banker. They had four children. Only one child, Jeanie, lived to grow up.

Baldwin was a Whig. Then he went to the meeting in Jackson in 1854 and became a Republican. Seven years later he was elected to the Michigan Senate.

While in the senate, Baldwin investigated the missing funds in the state treasury. (They came up missing when Moses Wisner was governor.) Baldwin was a banker and knew about finances. He made a report. He wrote rules so it couldn't happen again.

His wife, Harriet, died. Two years later he married Sibyl Lambard. She was 25 years younger than he was. They had three daughters; Sybil, Katharine and Marie.

In 1868, Baldwin ran for governor. He won by a big vote. He served two terms.

During his years in office there were two big forest fires in Michigan. One started in Holland. Another started in Manistee. Thousands of people were left homeless.

Baldwin gave a lot of his own money to help the homeless people. He also gave a lot of money to his church in Detroit.

After he was governor, Baldwin went back to business in Detroit. He built a big mansion. Eleven years after he was governor, he was appointed to the U.S. Senate. He was in Washington more than a year. He wanted to go back, but did not win the next election.

Baldwin died on December 31, 1892 in Detroit. He was 78 years old. Their beautiful mansion was torn down in 1943.

GOVERNOR JOHN J. BAGLEY
1873 THROUGH 1876

John Judson Bagley had seven brothers and sisters. He was born on July 24, 1832 in Medina, New York.

His father was a tanner. Tanners make animal hides into leather. He moved his family to Constantine, Michigan when John was eight years old.

By the time he was 14, John was earning his own living. He was a clerk in a country store. After a year, he left for Owosso. He was going to go to school there. But he soon left school and got a job as a clerk in a store.

When he was 16, John decided to go to Detroit. He was a big boy for his age. He didn't have any money. He wanted to see Detroit. When he got to the big city he liked it. He got a job in a tobacco factory. He worked in the factory until he was 21. Then he started his own tobacco business.

Bagley married Frances Newberry in Iowa. She came back to Detroit with him. At first they lived in a small house. They had eight children. His business grew fast. It was the largest of its kind in the West. He was one of the first businessmen to advertise.

He used his profits to get into other businesses. He was a good businessman. He made a fortune.

The Bagleys built a mansion in Detroit. He was president of the commission in charge of the Detroit Police Department. He was a Whig, but went to Jackson and joined the Republican party when it was formed.

In 1872 he was elected governor on the Republican ticket. He served two terms. Bagley ran the state government like a business. He set up new boards to run things. He changed the state militia to the National Guard.

Bagley was a big man with a big heart. He loved fountains. He had one built on the lawn of the state school in Coldwater. It was in memory of Kittie, his little daughter who died.

He came within one vote of running for the U.S. Senate in 1881. But his health was not good. He went to California to get better. It didn't help. He died in San Francisco, on July 27, 1881.

In his will, Bagley left money for a great big fountain in Detroit. He wanted people to drink cold, pure water from his fountain.

GOVERNOR CHARLES M. CROSWELL
1877 THROUGH 1880

Charles Croswell's father was a paper-maker. His name was John and he did business in New York City. His mother was Sallie Hicks. They lived in Newburg, New York. They had one daughter and one son, Charles. He was born on October 31, 1825.

When he was seven years old his mother and sister both died. Three months later his father drowned in the Hudson River.

Now Charles was an orphan and penniless. His Aunt Mary and Uncle Daniel Hicks took him in. When he was 12, they brought him to Adrian, Michigan. It was 1837, the year Michigan became a state.

Uncle Daniel was a carpenter. He started building houses in Adrian. When Charles was 16, he began to learn the carpenter's trade. For four years he worked to pay for his room and board. He spent his spare time reading and studying.

Then Charles Croswell was named Deputy Clerk of Lenawee County. He could work and study law at the same time. He became a lawyer. In 1850, he was elected Register of Deeds. He ran on the Whig ticket. He must have done a good job. He was re-elected.

Things were looking good. Croswell married Lucy Eddy in 1852. Two years later he went to Jackson for a political meeting. He was secretary of the meeting when they formed the Republican party.

In Adrian, Croswell was a law partner with Judge Thomas Cooley. (Cooley Law School in Lansing is named for him.) Within the next few years Croswell was mayor of Adrian. He was elected to the Michigan Senate three times. He was also elected president of the 1867 Constitutional Convention.

Then new sadness came to him. His wife, Lucy, fell down the stairs. She had their baby girl in her arms. Lucy died the next day. The baby lived. Lucy's parents came to take care of the children. They stayed for 12 years.

Croswell was a good writer. He was a good speaker. He knew how to conduct meetings. He was elected to the House of Representatives in 1872.

In 1876 he was the Republican candidate for governor. He won the election. He won

the next election, too. But just before he took office the second time, he remarried.

He married Elizabeth Musgrave from Eaton County. She was 25. He was 52. They lived in Lansing while he was governor.

During his term a great riot took place in Jackson. Railroad workers went on strike. Croswell sent troops in and saved lives. When he left office the budget was balanced. He went back to Adrian and tended to his business. He also helped buy the Opera House. It is known today as the Croswell Opera House.

Six years later, Croswell died on December 13, 1886. Three months after he died, Elizabeth had their only child. She named the baby Salliehicks, for Croswell's mother.

Years later Elizabeth gave their house to the D.A.R. association. They keep it as a memorial to Governor Croswell in Adrian.

GOVERNOR DAVID H. JEROME
1881 AND 1882

Until David Jerome became governor, all Michigan Governors had been born in the east. David was born in Detroit.

His mother and father came from New York to Detroit in 1827. David was born there on November 17, 1829. David was the youngest. He had seven brothers and sisters and five half-brothers and sisters. His father, Horace, and another man built the first lumber mill in the west. It was on Pine River in St. Clair County.

His father died when David was about a year old. His mother took him back with her to New York. When he was five years old she returned to Michigan and brought him with her. She raised him on a farm in St. Clair County.

David graduated from St. Clair Academy when he was 16. Then he did some logging. He rafted logs down the river. Soon David and his brother went into business. They chartered a steamer to run between Port Huron and Detroit.

They made good money hauling passengers and freight. But they tried to raise a ship that had sunk in Lake St. Clair. They lost all their money.

By then David was 19 and he decided to go to California. He worked for a mining company for a year. Then he came back to Michigan.

He started a general store in Saginaw. He changed it to a hardware store and it was the biggest one in the Saginaw Valley. He got into the lumber business with his half-brother. They became very wealthy.

In 1859, David married Lucy Amelia Peck from Oakland County. They were a good-looking couple. They had three children but only one lived. His name was Thomas Jerome and he grew up to be a lawyer in Detroit.

David Jerome didn't go to Jackson, but he was a charter member of the Republican party. He was elected a Michigan Senator on the party ticket in 1862 and re-elected two times.

Governor Blair asked him to raise a regiment for the Civil War. He prepared the men for duty. He became Colonel Jerome.

He was a Military Aide to Governor Crapo while he was in office.

Jerome loved adventure. He got it when he was appointed to the U.S. Board of Indian Commissioners. In 1876, he went with a delegation to see Chief Joseph on a peace mission. They traveled more than 600 miles up the Columbia River.

When he got back to Michigan he ran for governor. He was elected in 1880. Another bad forest fire broke out in September 1881. The fires swept across the part of Michigan that looks like a thumb. Some people had to get right into Lake Huron to keep from burning. More than 125 people were killed. Thousands were left homeless. The Red Cross came to help them. This was their first project.

When the next election came up, a new party was formed. It was the "Fusion" ticket and Josiah Begole won. Jerome lost. He went back to Saginaw and was president of two railroad companies.

Jerome was 67 years old when he went to a sanitarium at Watkins Glen, New York. Lucy went with him. He died there on April 23, 1896.

GOVERNOR JOSIAH W. BEGOLE
1883 AND 1884

When he was 21, Josiah Begole left New York for Michigan territory. He wanted to make his fortune. But he started out the hard way. He walked.

He came by steamer to Toledo. He walked from there to Jackson and then on to Flint. It was a long walk but he saved the $100 he had with him. It was all the money he had in the world. He didn't know how long it would last.

Josiah was born on January 20, 1815, in Livingston, New York. He was the oldest child in the family. He went to school in a log school house. Then he went to an Academy at Geneseo, New York. His parents had nine other children to raise. So when Josiah was 21, he was on his own.

There were only three or four houses in the village when he got to Flint. Josiah helped build houses in the summers. He taught school for two winters. Then a pretty girl came from New York. Josiah courted her. They were soon married in her family's log house. It was one of the first weddings in the wilderness. There was lots of excitement.

Josiah had bought some uncleared land. They began housekeeping in the woods. For 18 years they worked until it was a 500-acre farm. During this time they had five children: Mary, William, Frank, Charles and a baby girl who died.

Begole took time to be in local government. He had been a Whig, but was strong against slavery. He joined the Republican party.

During the Civil War he sent supplies to the army. His eldest son, William, was killed in the war. It was a great sadness in his life. He looked out for other families of soldiers.

As the years went by, Begole became wealthy. He owned one of Flint's largest sawmills. He was a banker and a businessman.

In 1871, he was elected a Michigan Senator. He served one term. Then he was elected to the U.S. Congress. He went to Washington for two years. He voted to have lots of green paper money made. He became known as a "Greenbacker."

After he came back to Flint, the Greenbackers and Democrats joined to form a Fusion party. He was their candidate for governor. He won and Republican Jerome lost.

Begole was 68. He was the oldest man ever elected Governor of Michigan. He was the only Fusionist ever elected, too. In the next election a Republican, Russell Alger beat him.

He returned to his businesses in Flint. He died on June 6, 1896. He was a true pioneer in Michigan.

GOVERNOR RUSSELL A. ALGER
1885 AND 1886

When Russell Alger was governor he was rich. He had a railroad car to haul him around. It was called the "Michigan."

But he knew what it was to be poor.

He was born in a log cabin at Lafayette, Ohio. on February 27, 1836. He had a younger brother and sister. Both their parents died when Russell was 11 years old. They were orphans. He found places for his brother and sister to live. But where could he go?

Russell's uncle gave him room and board for working on his farm. When he was 14, he became a farm laborer. He saved his money to pay tuition to school in the winters. As soon as he could, he got a job teaching school. Then he helped his brother and sister go to school.

When he was 21, he began to study law in Akron Ohio. He passed the bar exam in 1859 and then he moved to Cleveland. All the years of working and studying long hours had left him in poor health. He decided to come to Grand Rapids, Michigan.

Alger wanted to get into the lumber business. He did well at first. But a depression came and he went into debt. He met beautiful Annette Huldana Henry. They were married in her parents' home on April 2, 1861, in Grand Rapids.

Within weeks Civil War was declared. By August, Alger had become a private in the Cavalry. He was in 66 battles. He was taken prisoner of war, but he escaped. He was a war hero and he was a General by the time he came home.

Alger and Annette moved to Detroit. He got back in the lumber business. This time it was a success. He built railroads and iron industries. He became a multi-millionaire.

The Republican party got him to run for governor on its ticket. He won over Fusionist Josiah Begole. The Algers moved to Lansing. They had nine children, but only six were living now. They were Fay, Caroline, Frances, Russell Jr., Fred and Allen.

Alger ran the government like it was a business. He always looked out for veterans of the wars. When his term ended, he refused to run for re-election. The family

went back to Detroit. They lived in their big, beautiful mansion.

Then public service called again. Alger was appointed Secretary of War and went to Washington. He resigned after two years and came back to Detroit. He planned to stay there the rest of his life.

But three years later he was appointed to be in the U.S. Senate. Then he was elected for a six year term. He almost made it. Only a few weeks before his term was over, he died on January 24th, 1907, in Washington.

GOVERNOR CYRUS G. LUCE
1887 THROUGH 1890

Cyrus was the second son and one of six children in the Luce family. His father was a Yankee and his mother was from the south. They lived in Ohio when Cyrus was born on July 2, 1824.

They had to clear stumps from their farm land. Cyrus was needed to help as soon as he was big enough. He walked along a trail cut through the woods to get to a country school.

The family moved to Indiana when Cyrus was 12. He got a job driving a freight team to Toledo and back. He used the money he earned to pay tuition to an academy. He had to get up early to study. He worked all day. Then he stayed up late at night to study.

After three years of this, he finished school. Then he began working for his father in his business. They

40

made cloth by carding wool. Cyrus was in charge of the factory after seven years.

Some of his friends put his name up for election to the Indiana Legislature. Cyrus was 24 years old. He didn't know anything about politics. He lost the election.

He felt so bad that he took off for Michigan. He bought 80-acres of land near Coldwater. For a year he chopped trees and built a frame house. Then he married a neighbor girl, Julia Dickinson.

Luce was still interested in government. He was a county supervisor for 11 years. He was a Whig but was against slavery. So he went to the meeting in Jackson in 1854 and became a Republican.

He was elected to the House of Representatives for two years. Then he was elected two times to the Michigan Senate. He was a senator for four years. After this he was appointed the state oil inspector.

Luce always kept on farming. He joined the Michigan State Grange. It was started to help farmers. He was Master of the Grange for seven years.

During this time his wife, Julia, died. Four of their five children were still living. A year later he married Mary Brown Thompson. She was a widow, 19 years younger than he was. She and his children became good friends.

In 1886 the Republicans wanted a farmer to run for governor. They picked Cyrus Luce. He won the election. He and Mary

moved to Lansing. He took his horse and a cow to Lansing with them. He did the chores.

Luce was re-elected to another two-year term. He got laws passed to help farmers. He made sure that state money was well spent. He once traveled for three days to see if a prisoner should be pardoned. He found out the man had lied.

When his four years as governor ended, Luce and Mary went back to Coldwater. They bought a house in town. He took care of his businesses. His son ran his farm.

Luce died when he was 80 years old, on March 18, 1905. The Michigan Legislature held a Memorial Exercise for him in Lansing.

GOVERNOR EDWIN B. WINANS
1891 AND 1892

Edwin Winans was an only child. He was born on May 16, 1826 in Avon, New York. When he was eight years old his parents brought him to Michigan. They settled on a farm in Unadilla Township, Livingston County.

Then his father died. There was no one to help them. So Edwin and his mother moved to a nearby village. Edwin got a job in a wool-carding company.

He worked days and studied at home. When he was 20 years old he went to Albion College. He hoped to go to law school.

But the gold bug bit him in 1850. Gold was discovered out west and Edwin left for California. He didn't discover any gold mines. But he made money selling water to the miners. Then he and a partner opened a bank in the mining town of Rough and Ready. He made more money.

Five years after he'd left Michigan he came back. He wanted to marry the girl he'd left behind. Her name was Sarah Galloway. But Sarah didn't want to go to California.

"Take Lib," she said and pointed to her sister, Elizabeth.

Edwin liked Lib, too. So he asked her to marry him.

Lib said "Sure." She wanted to go to California.

They were married and headed back to Rough and Ready. They lived there three years. They had a little boy and named him George. Then they came back to Michigan. They lived on Lib's parents farm near Hamburg.

Edwin Winans went back out west one more time. He went to Idaho. He hauled supplies on wagons to sell to the pioneers. He sold the wagons, too, and took the stagecoach for home. On the way the stagecoach overturned. His gun went off and he was hit with his own buckshot. It was several months before he was well. When he got back to Hamburg he decided to stay there.

He bought the Galloway 400-acre farm. He had to learn how to farm. While moving a boulder, he strained one eye. It had to be removed. He had to wear a glass eye the rest of his life.

Winans was soon interested in politics. He was a Democrat in a Republican area. But people liked him. They elected him to the House of Representatives in 1860. They re-elected him in 1862. Then he came back to the farm for five years. He left only to take part in the 1867 Constitutional Convention.

Winans and Lib built a big new house. It was by a lake on their farm. The lake became Winans Lake. They had another son. His name was Edwin Jr.

About 10 years after he'd been to the Constitutional Convention, Winans ran for Judge of Probate in his county. He said he wanted a handle on his name before he died. He won the election and became Judge Winans. He liked the handle but he didn't like the job. He was glad when the four-year term was over.

Winans kept going to the Democrat's meetings. They picked him to run for Congress. No one else would run. They didn't think a Democrat could win the election. A friend behind Winans held his coattail so he couldn't get up. They ended the meeting before he could say, "No."

He decided to work hard and win the election. He did. He went to Washington and did a good job. He was re-elected two years later, in 1884.

By now the Democrats wanted to run a farmer for governor. They nominated Winans in 1890. Many Republicans liked him, too. He won the election. It was the first time a Democrat had been elected governor in 40 years.

Winans weighed about 200 pounds. He had a sense of humor. He didn't like drinking or swearing. He tried to save money for the state when he was governor. His son, George, was his secretary in the Capitol. His other son, Edwin, graduated from West Point.

Winans went home to his farm as often as he could. He became known as the "Farmer Governor." It was Governor Luce who spent his life farming. But Winans got the title.

He didn't run for a second term. Winans went back to his farm. He died there 18 months later, on the Fourth of July in 1894. He was 68 years old. He'd led a busy life.

GOVERNOR JOHN T. RICH
1893 THROUGH 1896

Little John Rich was the only child of John and Jerusha Rich. He was born when they lived in Pennsylvania (April 23, 1841) but they moved to Vermont when he was five years old.

A year later his mother died. John's father had brothers and sisters who lived in Lapeer. So he brought little John with him to Michigan. They settled on land in Elba Township, not far from Lapeer. The country was new. There was an Indian reservation in the township.

The land had to be cleared before they could raise crops on it. It was a lonesome time for the two of them. John's uncles in Vermont had raised sheep. He liked them too. Then John's father married a woman from Atlas, Anna Winship. She had eight brothers and sisters.

44

John went to the red schoolhouse about a mile from their farm. Then he went to an academy in Clarkston. Next he went to school in the village of Lapeer. But he had to leave school and go back to work on the farm.

John Rich was friendly and modest. He was a big man. They didn't call him little John anymore. When he was 22 years old he married one of his step-mother's sisters. Her name was Lucretia. She was about five years older than he was. They never had any children but they had lots of nieces and nephews.

A few years after he was married, Rich was elected township supervisor. From then on he was in Republican politics. He was re-elected supervisor three more times. Then he was elected to the State House of Representatives. When he went to Lansing, Lucretia went with him. They stayed in a hotel there. He was re-elected three more times.

Rich did such a good job he was elected in 1880 to the Michigan Senate. Before his term was up he was elected to Congress. Lucretia went with him to Washington, too.

He didn't get re-elected to Congress, though. They came back to their farm. A nephew was running it for them. Rich didn't stay on the farm long. Two times he was nominated to run for governor but someone else was picked. He was named the State Commissioner of Railroads and made a fine record.

In 1892, Rich got the nomination for governor. He won the election. He and Lucretia moved back to Lansing. His first year in office was a hard one. Some state officials weren't honest and Rich fired them. And there was a depression. Banks closed. Mines closed in the Upper Peninsula. People were out of jobs.

But things began to get better. More people voted for Rich the second time than the first time. He got the State Home for Feeble Minded built in Lapeer.

When his second term was done, Rich and Lucretia went back to their farm again. He wanted to be there with his Merino sheep. He was president of the State Fair. But new governors needed his help. He was appointed to be collector of customs in Detroit and at Port Huron. Then he was appointed State Treasurer. State money had disappeared and the Governor asked Rich to find it. He cleaned up the books.

By now Lucretia wasn't well. They lived with her sister near the railroad depot in Elba. It was easier for John T. to go back and forth on business. Lucretia died in 1912. Three years later, Rich married her niece, Georgia Winship.

Rich kept farming but spent winters in Florida. He was almost 85 years old when he died there on March 28, 1926.

GOVERNOR HAZEN S. PINGREE
1897 THROUGH 1900

Hazen Pingree was called "Ping." He worked on his father's farm when he was a boy. The land was poor and it was hard to make a living. Ping never forgot. He always tried to help poor people.

Ping was born in Maine on August 30, 1830. He was the fourth child in the family. They all worked on the farm and went to the country school in the winters.

When Ping was 14, he left home to work in a cotton factory. He missed his family. Six years later he got a job in Massachusetts. He was a shoe cutter in a shoe factory. The Civil War broke out and Ping joined up in 1862. He was a private. He was in many battles and was captured by Mosby's Raiders. They kept him a prisoner of war for five months.

When the war was over, Ping came to Detroit. He got a job working for Henry Baldwin's boot and shoe factory. (Henry Baldwin later became a Michigan Governor.)

Ping and a partner bought a small shoe business. It became one of the biggest shoe companies in the west. He began building a mansion in Detroit. He married a school teacher from Mt. Clemens. Her name was Frances Gilbert. They had three children. Gertrude, Hazen Jr. (called Joe), and Hazel. Gertrude died when she was a teenager.

The Pingrees had lots of friends. Most of them owned businesses in Detroit. They wanted Ping to run for Mayor of Detroit. He was elected. Then he surprised them. He made the companies lower the horsecar fare from five cents to three cents. He made them lower their prices for electricity and gas.

The owners of the companies were angry. They wouldn't come to Pingree's house anymore. This made Mrs. Pingree sad. She wouldn't go places with him. She stayed at home all the time.

A Panic in 1893 left a lot of people hungry. Ping got property owners to let them plant gardens. He sold his horse to buy seeds and tools for the people. They called him "Potato-Patch Pingree."

While he was mayor the Republicans asked him to run for governor. They knew the people would vote for him. And, if he was governor he would leave Detroit.

Old Ping got elected in 1896. He decided to be mayor and governor, too. The Michigan Supreme Court told him he couldn't be both. He quit being mayor.

In Lansing, Ping wanted to do more things to help the common people. The legislators didn't agree with him. He made them come back to Lansing many times for special meetings. When they came back they still wouldn't pass the laws he wanted. Years later his ideas did get into laws.

The Spanish-American War broke out while Ping was governor. He had been a soldier and he knew what it was like. He lived with the soldiers in their camp near Brighton. He visited camps down south and saw they got better food. He sent nurses to help the wounded. He sent trains to bring the soldiers back home.

Ping was re-elected governor. He kept trying to make things better for the people. Like lowering their taxes. Almost everyone else was against him. When he left Lansing as governor he headed for Africa. He went to hunt elephants.

On the way home he got sick and died in England. He died on June 18, 1901. He was 60 years old. Ping's funeral was the biggest one Detroit ever had. A statue was put up for him. It calls him the "Idol of the People.

GOVERNOR AARON T. BLISS
1901 THROUGH 1904

Aaron Bliss had six brothers and two sisters. His family was very poor. They lived on a farm near Smithfield in New York State. He was born on May 22, 1837. His mother was Anna and his father was Lyman Bliss.

Aaron went to the little red school house nearby. He worked on the farm until he was 17. Then he left home to work in a store. He worked more than a year for $100.

He moved to another town and was a clerk in a store there. In three years he was made a partner. Then the Civil War broke out. The partners sold the store and had just enough money to pay their debts.

Aaron was 20 years old. He joined the cavalry. He got other men to join, too. They had to bring their own horses. He was promoted to sergeant, first lieutenant and then to captain. They went south to fight in the war.

He was captured by the Confederate soldiers. He was put on a train. He and two other soldiers had a case knife. They sawed a hole in the bottom of the railroad car. When the train stopped they got away. Bloodhounds chased them and they climbed a tree. The Confederates came and caught them.

They were sent to a prison and tried to tunnel out. They were caught again. They were sent to other prisons and finally Aaron escaped. He spent 18 days and 19 nights in the woods. He nearly starved. He only had three ears of raw corn to eat for three days. Then he found the Union lines and was safe. He was ragged, thin and dirty. His health was poor. He resigned from the army in February 1865. He had been in the army three and a half years.

One of his brothers, Dr. Lyman Bliss had come to Saginaw, Michigan. Aaron decided to come, too. He was called "Cap" Bliss. He was still not very strong. He had no sense of humor and no time to tell a funny story. He worked hard in a lumber camp. He saved his money and bought a lot of timber land. He went into business with his brother.

Aaron went back to New York and married a girl he'd known in school. Allaseba Phelps was her name. She came to live in

his lumbercamp and cooked for the lumberjacks. In a few years they made a lot of money.

Aaron and Allaseba moved into Saginaw. They lived in the barn while their house was built. It was a beautiful house. Allaseba gave fancy parties there.

"I never wanted to go into politics," Aaron Bliss said later. But he was elected to the Michigan Senate. Then the Republican party wanted him to run for Congress. He did and he won. Allaseba went with him to Washington, D.C. He didn't get re-elected and they came back to Saginaw. They never had any children.

In 1900 Aaron Bliss was elected Governor of Michigan. He got the government to save money. He was a good businessman but not a good judge of people. They took advantage of him. He was not a good speaker. But he was elected a second time. When he left office, Michigan had money in the bank.

About a year after being governor, Bliss had a stroke. He died in a sanitarium in Wisconsin on September 16, 1906. He was 69 years old.

GOVERNOR FRED M. WARNER
1905 THROUGH 1910

Fred Maltby was a tiny baby when his mother and father brought him to Michigan. He was born in England on July 21, 1865. His two sisters came with them. His older brother stayed in England with relatives.

They settled on a farm in Livonia Township. But soon his mother died. His father could not raise them alone. He put the girls out to live with other families. Who would take a baby?

Rhoda and P.D. Warner lived in Farmington. They didn't have any children of their own. They had adopted a little girl, Mary, who was now seven years old. They said they would keep baby Fred for a week. He was a good little baby. They decided he would be their boy. When he was seven months old they adopted him.

The Warner's loved Fred very much. One time Rhoda was holding him and said, "I am afraid this boy will never amount to anything." P.D. laughed and said, "If he lives to be 40 years old he will be six feet tall and weigh 200 pounds."

(On his 40th birthday he was six feet tall, weighed 203 pounds and was Governor of Michigan.)

P.D. owned a general store. He was a state legislator and respected. He built a big, new house when Freddy was four years old. (Later on this became Fred's house and today it is a museum.)

Freddy went to the village school. He was very shy. He would cry when he was asked to recite. His sister would hold his hand. If she let go, he would cry again. He was a good speller, but not so good at hand-writing.

When Freddy was 11, P.D. took him to the United States Centennial Exhibition in Philadelphia. He kept a diary of the trip. He counted the steps up to buildings. He saw many new things.

When he was 14, P.D. took him to Europe. They visited the town in England where Fred was born. They went to church. They were gone more than two months. P.D. wanted Fred to see and learn as much as he could.

In 1880, Fred was sent to Michigan Agricultural College in Lansing. He only stayed one semester. Then he came back to work in his father's store. He liked to ride a bicycle. He saved his money and bought a high-wheeled bicycle. He entered races and won State Championships.

P.D. turned his store business over to Fred when he was 21. A year later Fred married Martha Davis. They had five children but one of them died. They lived in the big house that P.D. had built.

Fred decided to go into the cheese business. He built a cheese "factory" on their 250-acre farm. It did so well that in nine years he had more than 12 cheese factories. He called the business the Warner Dairy Company.

He also liked politics. He was on the village council for ten years. Then he was a Michigan Senator for four years. Next he ran for Secretary of State and was elected two times. People around the state got to know him. When he ran for governor in 1904, they voted for him. He was re-elected two times. He was the first governor to hold three terms in a row.

Many laws were passed to help people while Fred Warner was governor. Afterwards, he went back to his farming and businesses. He wasn't well, though. He went to a sanatorium in Florida. He was 57 years old. He had hoped to get better there, but he died on April 17, 1923.

GOVERNOR CHASE S. OSBORN
1911 AND 1912

When Chase Osborn was a boy, he did his own thing. He never changed very much.

He was born in a log house in Huntington County, Indiana. It was on January 22, 1860. He had seven brothers and sisters. His mother, Margaret Ann, and his father, George, were both doctors. She was one of the first women doctors in the nation.

Chase was a runaway boy. But he was a smart little fellow. He always knew enough to come home.

He went to school in nearby Lafayette. He sold newspapers to earn money. He learned to set type in the print shop. He liked this work.

Chase spent three years at Purdue University. But he liked the newspaper work best. He came back to work at the *Lafayette Home Journal*.

Before long Chase left for Chicago to work on the *Chicago Tribune*. Then he moved to the *Milwaukee Sentinel* in Wisconsin. He ran on his assignments and carried a hatchet in his belt. He was a young man in a hurry.

In Milwaukee, Chase met and married Lillian Jones. They didn't have much money to live on. He earned $12 a week.

A year later he bought a newspaper of his own in Florence, Wisconsin. He made it pay. Then he sold it. He bought the *Sault Ste. Marie Evening News* in the Upper Peninsula of Michigan.

The paper began to make money. The Osborns had seven children. Three of them died before they were five years old. They built a big house. Chase bought riding horses. Then he decided it was better to walk. He gave the horses away.

Chase loved the outdoors. He loved to hike. He liked to travel. And he was interested in politics. Governors appointed him to special jobs. He was the State Fish and Game Warden. Next he was the State Railroad Commissioner.

In 1900 he decided to run for governor. He didn't get very far. The men running against him were millionaires. So Chase sold his paper and bought part of another one in Saginaw. He tramped around the Upper Peninsula and found an iron deposit. It was called the Moose Mountain iron range. He made a pile of money.

In 1910 he ran again for governor. He traveled all over the state. A newspaper said that Chase needed a rest. "He kicks and throws bricks at everyone." But this time he won.

He had many ideas and some of them got passed into laws. Most of the legislators didn't like his ideas. He wanted to make progress. They wanted to keep things the way they were. He went to visit his old hometown in Indiana. An old neighbor shook his hand. "Ain't you been hanged yet?" he asked Chase.

He had promised to make government less expensive. He did. He had promised to be governor only one term. So when two years were up, he didn't run for re-election. Later, he said he'd had the time of his life when he was governor.

After Chase left Lansing he took trips all over the world. He ran for governor again in 1914, but was traveling most of the time. He didn't win the election.

In the last 20 years of his life, Chase worked to see Isle Royale become a national park. It did. He wanted to get a bridge built

between lower and upper Michigan. It didn't happen until many years later.

He and a young boy in Traverse City wrote letters to each other. Chase put a dollar in each letter he sent. The boy was William Milliken.

Chase liked to sleep outdoors at his camp in Possom Poke in Georgia. He liked to spend time at his camp on Duck Island in the Upper Peninsula. He wrote many books and gave most of his money to universities and colleges.

Chase Osborn died on April 11, 1949. He was buried on Duck Island. Years later, Osborn's portrait hung on the wall across from the Governor's office in Lansing. The Governor took good care of it. He was William Milliken.

GOVERNOR WOODBRIDGE N. FERRIS
1913 THROUGH 1916

There were eight children in Woodbridge Ferris' family. His mother, Estella, and his father, John, were very poor. They had about 75 acres of land in New York State. It was covered with trees. They cut the trees down and built a cabin with the logs.

Woodbridge Nathan was born in the log cabin on January 6, 1853. As he grew up he helped clear the land and plant crops. They had little patches of corn and wheat. A few cows gave them milk to drink. A few sheep gave them wool so his mother could make them warm clothes.

Woodbridge was sent to school when he was four years old. He had one reader for two years. He could not have a slate to write on because the teacher was afraid he would draw pictures. He got bored. He got into mischief and often got flogged.

He liked to be outdoors. He liked to play baseball, snap-the-whip, and he learned to swim. In the winter he played fox-and-geese and ice-skated. He liked to hunt with his father's old musket. He hunted squirrel, partridge and quail for the family to eat. He also trapped woodchuck. In those days they ate woodchuck.

When he was 14, Woodbridge went to the Spencer Union Academy. It was in the nearby village of Spencer. He was unhappy here. The other children made fun of his clothes. His manners were different, too.

His teacher called him a blockhead he was so poor in grammar. But he studied and got better. When he was 16, he was glad to go to Candor Union academy. He roomed with another boy and they cooked their own meals. He worked summers on a farm to pay his expenses.

When he was 17, he went to a Teacher's Institute. He got a certificate to teach. From then on he taught in winters and worked on farms summers. He saved his money so he could get more education. He took courses at the Oswego Academy and met a pretty, smart girl. Her name was Helen Gillespie.

He came to study medicine at the University of Michigan. He always read medical books. But he decided to make teaching his life work. He went back to Spencer Academy to teach. He and Helen were married. She taught there, too.

They wanted to start their own school. They wanted to teach students skills so they could get jobs. They organized business schools in New York State and in Illinois. Then, in 1884 they moved to Big Rapids, Michigan. They started the Ferris Industrial School. (It is now Ferris State University.)

As the school grew, so did their family. By now they had two sons. (A third son had died when he was a baby.) Woodbridge became president of a bank in Big Rapids. He could manage money. They owned a big farm and he raised cattle there. He also liked to work in his gardens.

The Democrats wanted him to run for an office. He ran for Congress in 1892 and lost. He ran for governor in 1904 and lost again. Eight years later he ran for governor and this time he won.

By now, graduates of his school were living all over the state. They had worked to get him elected. He went to Lansing but Helen was sick and stayed home. He wrote to her every day.

Woodbridge got along well with the legislators. When a strike broke out in the Upper Peninsula, he sent the entire National Guard to keep order. He was re-elected for two more years. Then he went back to Big Rapids. He was happy to teach again. But he was sad when Helen died a few months later.

In 1920, Woodbridge Ferris ran for governor again, but he lost. In 1922 he ran for the U.S. Senate. He went all over the state, smoked big black cigars and talked to people. He won the election and went to Washington, D.C.

For nearly six years there he used common sense. He was known for his honesty. And he always went to Senate meetings, even when he was sick. He should have stayed in bed like the doctor said. He died on March 23, 1928. He was 75 years old.

GOVERNOR ALBERT E. SLEEPER
1917 THROUGH 1920

"Uncle Bert" Sleeper was governor during World War I. The war began soon after he became governor. It lasted nearly two years, from April 6, 1917 to November 11, 1918. By the time he left office the war was over.

Albert Edson Sleeper was born in Vermont on December 31, 1862. He was the son of Joseph Edson and Hannah Sleeper. He studied at Bradford Academy.

When he was 21 years old he left Vermont and came to Lexington, Michigan. He came to work in his uncle's dry goods store. He was a buyer and a manager of the store. It was one of the largest in the state. He became a traveling salesman for the store. He was friendly. He met a lot of people on his trips.

Bert had a knack for business. Within 16 years he was president of four banks and a grocery company.

He was president of Lexington village. He was a Republican. He ran for the Michigan Senate and was elected twice, in 1901 and 1903. He rode the train back and forth to Lansing to work in the senate.

Bert Sleeper and Mary Charlotte Moore were married on July 30, 1901. They moved to nearby Bad Axe. They lived there the rest of their lives. They never had any children of their own. But a friend came to visit them from Vermont and he died while he was here in Michigan. He had four children. Bert and Mary were very sorry. They loved children.

They had the children come and spend their summers with them. Two of the children, Phoebe and Stevens, came to live with them all the time. They called him Uncle Bert.

After Sleeper was in the senate, he was elected State Treasurer. He was treasurer for Governor Warner and Governor Osborn. He kept good books. They were glad he was their treasurer.

In 1916 he ran for governor and was elected. By now more people had automobiles and the Sleepers bought one. The roads weren't good though. They often got stuck in the mud. It cost them $10 to get pulled out by farmers with horses.

Uncle Bert loved new cars. Stevens drove for him. They liked to go to Detroit to see the Auto shows.

World War I broke out and there wasn't much gas. They rode the trains again. They went to Camp Custer near Battle Creek to see the soldiers. Sleeper was busy getting food and supplies from Michigan to the U.S. Army.

Thousands of people got sick and died with the flu. Stores and churches were closed so the flu wouldn't spread. There wasn't much coal. People were cold. It was a hard time for everyone.

The war ended on November 11, 1918. Armistice Day. (Now it's called Veteran's Day.) Everyone was happy. They danced in the streets. The soldiers came home.

Sleeper had been elected governor again. He tried to get things back to normal. His attorney general did not help Sleeper. He wanted to be governor himself. Sure enough, the attorney general ran for governor next time. His name was Alex Groesbeck and he won the election.

The Sleepers had a nice home in Bad Axe. He went back to his businesses. He helped the Republicans get rid of Governor Groesbeck.

When the Great Depression hit in 1929, Sleeper lost a lot of money. Still, he always helped people who needed help. Sleeper died on May 13, 1934. He was 71 years old.

There is a state park named for him near his old home. It is the Albert E. Sleeper State Park.

ALEXANDER J. GROESBECK
1921 THROUGH 1926

It is a puzzle how Alexander Groesback could get elected governor. Hardly anyone seemed to like him. The longer he was governor, the less they liked him. He shook up the government, but he made it run better. They respected him for this.

His grandfather was the first pioneer to settle in Macomb County. His father was Louis Groesback and his mother was Julia.

Alex, as he wanted to be called, was born in Warren Township on November 7, 1872 or 1873. (The records are different.) He was baptized Alexander Joseph at the St. Clement Roman Catholic Church.

When Alex was about 8 years old, his father was elected Macomb County Sheriff. The family moved to Mt. Clemens. Alex went to school there. Then they moved to Ontario, Canada, for two years. His father worked for a lumber company. Alex went to school at Wallaceburg, Ontario.

When he was 13, Alex started working in a sawmill. He worked there until he was 17. He had time to think. He decided he didn't want to work in a sawmill all his life. He wanted to be a lawyer.

He got a job with a law firm in Port Huron so he could study law. Then he went to the University of Michigan and studied some more. He graduated from the University of Michigan law school in 1893. He was a lawyer in Detroit for many years.

Alex got busy in the Republican party. The Republicans had a big fight in Bay City and he became their State Chairman (1912). Four years later he was elected Attorney General of Michigan. He was re-elected. He investigated many things and made news. His name became well known.

He was elected governor in 1920 and re-elected two more times. Alex never got married. He worked many hours in his office. He didn't like a lot of fuss. When he was sworn into office, he'd slip into the Capitol and slip back out. There were no big ceremonies.

Alex Groesbeck had highways built for cars to drive on. Until now the roads were often mud trails. He had prisoners work on the roads.

He set up a board to run the state government. He ran the government like a

business. Taxes were raised. He didn't let people know how much money was in the treasury. They wanted to take a peek at the budget.

More and more people said he was acting like a dictator. He fought with his best friend in politics. He said he was going to run for governor a fourth time. But the Republicans didn't let him. They nominated Fred Green and he won the election for governor.

Groesbeck went back to Detroit. He practiced law and made money in business. Two more times he tried to run for governor. The Republicans wouldn't nominate him. Then he said he'd never run for office again.

Later, he was appointed to a state board by a Democrat. Alex J. Groesbeck died on March 10, 1953 at the age of 79. Like him or not, he had worked for good government.

Governor Fred W. Green
1927 through 1930

Fred Green was raised in Cadillac. The land was wild and open. He loved to hunt and fish from the time he was a boy.

He was born in Manistee on October 20, 1872. His father was a lawyer and a lumberman. His mother and father brought Fred with them to Cadillac a year after he was born.

Fred was a happy boy and didn't worry about things. When he finished high school he went to college at Ypsilanti. He worked for the *Ypsilantian*, a Republican weekly newspaper. He got a degree to teach school. But he liked reporting so much that he stayed two years at the paper.

Then he went to law school at the University of Michigan. He sold insurance to pay his way. He dated

Helen Kelly who came from Cadillac to the University of Michigan, too. She went back to Cadillac to teach. He got his law degree and enlisted in the Army.

Fred was sent to Cuba in the Spanish-American war. He came home a first lieutenant. After his return he was appointed Inspector General of State Troops by Governor Hazen Pingree and later became a Brigadier General.

He began practicing law in Ypsilanti when he got back from the war. He owned part of the Ypsilanti Reed Furniture Company. He and Helen were married on June 18, 1901. He bought the other part of the furniture company and moved it to Ionia.

The furniture company grew to be the largest in the country. Fred got into other businesses, too. The Greens became very wealthy. They built a mansion on the bank of the Grand River. They had one child, a daughter named Helen Nancy.

Fred was mayor of Ionia for 13 years. He was treasurer of the Republican party for 10 years. In 1926 he was elected Governor of Michigan.

The story is told that Fred wore red wool socks the day he took office as governor. The ceremony was on the Capitol steps and everyone was all dressed up. It was a very cold day and he knew how to keep his feet warm. He was a hunter.

Now that he was governor, he remembered his friends. The author, James Oliver

Curwood of Owosso, was his friend. He put Curwood on the Conservation Commission to save wildlife in Michigan. (This is the DNR today.)

Fred Green didn't try to change things. He just ran the government. He was elected a second time. Then the stock market crashed in 1929. Some people lost all their money. But it was after Green left office that the Great Depression hurt everyone.

Green didn't run for a third term. He spent his time doing things he liked. His granddaughter lived with him and Helen. Her name was Helen, too. He bought her a pony and taught her to be a horse woman. They both loved horses.

Fred Green was in the Upper Peninsula at his hunting lodge when he got sick. His granddaughter said he died of peritonitis. He was 64 years old when he died on November 30, 1936.

GOVERNOR WILBER M. BRUCKER
1931 AND 1932

Wilber Brucker's father was a lawyer and a Democrat. His mother was a Republican. Wilber grew up to be a lawyer and a Republican.

The Brucker family lived in Saginaw when Wilber was born on June 23, 1894. He had three older brothers.

His father was a U.S. Congressman. When Wilber was four years old his father did not get re-elected to Congress. His father was sick for the next five years until he died.

"We were in pretty bad shape," Wilber said. "...it was tough." A schoolteacher aunt came to live with them. The boys all worked to help out.

Wilber pulled mustard weeds out of corn fields at a penny a row. He had other jobs while he went to school in Saginaw. When he graduated from high school in 1912, he went to the University of Michigan.

He worked to pay his way through law school. He spent summers in a Saginaw lumber yard. He waited on tables in Ann Arbor. He joined the National Guard.

As soon as Wilber graduated, he was called to service. He was sent to Mexico to fight Pancho Villa. When he got back home, World War I had started. He was sent to France with the "Rainbow" Division. He was a hero. He got a Silver Star for bravery and a Purple Heart for wounds. He was a first lieutenant when he came home.

Wilber opened his law office in Saginaw. It was so small he called it a cubby-hole. He married his sweetheart on August 18, 1923. She was Clara Hantel. Her father was a minister. They had waited eight years to get married.

Wilber Brucker joined the Republican party. He became Saginaw County Prosecutor. In 1927 he went to Lansing and the next year he was elected state attorney general. Three years later he ran for governor.

Brucker was 36 years old when he was elected governor. He was a good friend of President Herbert Hoover. They were fighting the Depression. Banks were closing, people were out of work.

Brucker tried to make jobs. He thought people wanted to work, not get handouts.

He started a big highway building program. But it took time. In 1932 Franklin D. Roosevelt won the election by a landslide. A Democrat Governor, William A. Comstock won the governorship in Michigan.

Clara, their little son Wilber II, and Brucker left Lansing and moved to Detroit. He joined a law firm and became very wealthy. They built a home in Grosse Pointe Farms.

Twenty years later President Dwight D. Eisenhower named Brucker to his cabinet. Brucker became Secretary of the Army for six years, until 1961. He and Clara traveled around the world. She kept notes and took pictures. She wrote a book about their life.

When he was 74 years old, Brucker died of a heart attack (October 28, 1968) in Detroit. He was buried in Arlington National Cemetery.

The United States Army Band building is named the Wilber M. Brucker Hall in his honor. It is at Fort Meyer, Virginia.

GOVERNOR WILLIAM A. COMSTOCK
1933 AND 1934

He was William A. and his father was William B. He liked to be called Bill Comstock.

Bill was born in Alpena on July 2, 1877. He had three sisters. His mother and father were rich. His father was a lumberman. Bill spent a great deal of time in the forests with his father. He liked to ride the logs on rivers up north. He worked in the woods with the lumberjacks. He became an expert woodsman.

He always loved the outdoors. He loved to hunt and fish.

Bill went to school in Alpena and worked for his father's electric railroad system. Then he went to the University of Michigan. He graduated in 1899, almost 100 years ago.

Today we might call him an egghead. He was very smart and he wore glasses. But we wouldn't be very smart to call him that because he was also a boxer. He boxed at the University and against professionals in Chicago.

Bill got his degree from the University of Michigan and came back to Alpena. He took over his father's business and became a millionaire. When World War I broke out, he went to serve in the army. He was discharged because of poor eyesight. So he helped the Red Cross.

Most people in Alpena were Republicans. Bill thought he'd have more opportunities as a Democrat. He was elected mayor of Alpena.

In 1919 he met Josephine White Morrison from Detroit. She had been married and had a son. Bill married her and adopted her son. Then they had a boy of their own, William Comstock III.

Bill Comstock then began pouring money into the Democratic party. It was almost dead. He kept it alive. No one knew how much money he gave. He let his name be put on their ticket for governor—three times. He knew a Democrat couldn't win.

Comstock was appointed a Regent of the University of Michigan. He liked this best of any of the offices he ever held.

In 1932, the Democrats had a chance to win an election in Michigan. Comstock had lost his millions in the Great Depression. He was broke now but he ran for governor again.

He won and was governor for two years. He behaved like a statesman. He was a gentleman.

These were hard times in Michigan and all over the country. Comstock had to close the banks. He got a sales tax passed. He set up programs to help the poor. But other Democrats said he didn't do enough. They wanted to have the federal government do more. They got into big fights.

When the 1934 election came around, the Democrats did not pick Comstock to run again for governor. It broke his heart. He'd lost millions of dollars but kept smiling. Now he was very sad because his party had let him down.

Later he was elected many times to offices in Detroit and Wayne County. He didn't run as a Democrat, though. He was nonpartisan.

As he grew older, Comstock had three strokes. When he was 71, he went to his hunting club near Alpena. He had another stroke and was taken to the hospital. He died three weeks later, on June 16, 1949.

GOVERNOR FRANK D. FITZGERALD

1935 AND 1936
JANUARY 1, 1939 TO MARCH 16, 1939

The one thing Frank Fitzgerald wanted most when he was a boy was a pony and a cart. So he began by trading marbles and a jack knife until he got one. Then he began a delivery service. He charged 10 cents to deliver things for people until he paid for the pony and cart.

He was like that all his life. He decided what he wanted. He planned how to get it and worked until he got it.

Frank was born on January 27, 1885, in Grand Ledge. He had an older sister, Pearl, and an older brother, Harry. His mother and father were Republicans. His father was elected a State Representative for

two years. He often took young Frank with him to Lansing.

Frank liked the big desk in the Capitol building where his father sat. There was a thick carpet on the floor and chandeliers hung above. It was awesome. He didn't forget.

He left high school before he graduated. Later, he was sorry he didn't stay to graduate. But he had a lot to do. He went to study business at Ferris Institute in Big Rapids.

During summer vacations Frank went out West to work on ranches. When he finished school he came back to Grand Ledge. He worked in the post office five years for his father. He met a girl named Queena Warner and they were married. They had one son.

When Frank Fitzgerald was 27, he ran for his first political office. He was elected a county supervisor. Then he got a job in Lansing, working in the Capitol. After a few years he was appointed business manager of the State Highway Department. He met a lot of people and made a lot of friends.

Fitzgerald was a tall man. He always wore neat clothes. He liked to go on hikes with his son and he liked to garden. The family led a quiet life in Grand Ledge. Everyone knew them and they knew everyone.

Before long Fitzgerald was running for another office. He was elected Secretary of State. He met more people and made more friends. He was re-elected to the office.

Then he ran for governor in 1934. He won the election and was governor for two years. Now he had the nicest office in the Capitol building. But he didn't get re-elected in 1936. Frank Murphy became governor instead.

Fitzgerald didn't like losing an election. He decided to run against Murphy two years later. He worked so hard that he wore himself out. Still, he won the election and was governor again.

Only 10 weeks after he was back in the Governor's office, Fitzgerald got sick. He was 54 years old when he died on March 16, 1939. He was the only Michigan governor to die while in office.

His son became a Michigan Supreme Court Justice and his grandson is a State Representative today.

GOVERNOR FRANK MURPHY
1937 AND 1938

Frank Murphy's real name was William Francis Murphy. He was called Frank and always used that name.

He was born on April 13, 1890, near Harbor Beach. His father was a lawyer. His mother was a school-teacher. He had an older brother, Harold. He had a younger brother George. He had one sister, Marguerite. The Murphys were Irish, Catholics and Democrats.

They lived behind his father's office. Then they bought a big house down the street. Frank was a red-haired Irishman. He was soft-hearted but he liked a good fight.

In high school he was a fairly good student. He played on the football and baseball and track teams. He was a star on the debate team.

When he graduated from high school his mother gave him a Bible. She wrote in it. "To dear Frank from Mamma on the day he graduated, June 26, 1908." He read the Bible every day. He went to Mass every Sunday.

Frank went to the University of Michigan. He worked summers to help pay his way. He dreamed of "ruling cities in our good land."

In law school he didn't do very well his first year. He passed only four of his eight courses. But he made up the classes and graduated with a law degree in 1914. He moved to Detroit.

When World War I started, Frank enlisted and went overseas. He was a captain in the infantry. When the war ended, he came back to Detroit. In a few years he became a federal attorney. He was hard on crooks but felt sorry for their families and tried to help them.

Frank was single and women chased him but he never got married. He didn't smoke nor drink. He wanted to be healthy so he could be in politics. He was elected a judge in Detroit. Six years later, in 1930, he was elected mayor of Detroit.

It was the time of the Great Depression. People were out of jobs and hungry. Frank Murphy did all he could to help them. People couldn't pay their taxes and the city ran out of money. The state didn't send money. He wanted the federal government to help. Frank worked to get votes for Franklin D. Roosevelt, a Democrat, for President. They became good friends.

Roosevelt won the election in 1933. To reward Frank for his help, he sent him to the Philippines to be governor-general. Frank's sister and her husband went with him. She went where he did from then on because he had no wife to help him.

In 1936 President Roosevelt called Frank back to Michigan to run for governor. Frank won. He was governor for two years. There was a strike in Flint. Frank got it settled peacefully. He liked the working men. The unions liked Frank.

There were more strikes. Now the people blamed Frank for not stopping the strikers. He didn't win the next election. President Roosevelt called him to Washington. He named Frank Murphy the Attorney General. Then he named him to be a Justice on the United States Supreme Court.

Murphy became the only man from Michigan to ever serve on the high court. He was a Justice from 1940 until July 1949. In July he was on his way to Harbor Beach for a vacation. He stopped in a Detroit hospital for a check-up. While he was there he had a heart attack and died. He was 59 years old. He was buried near Harbor Beach.

The house where Frank Murphy was born is a museum today.

GOVERNOR LUREN D. DICKINSON
1939 AND 1940

When Luren Dickinson was a year old, his mother and father brought him to Michigan. He was born in New York, April 12, 1859. They settled near Charlotte on a small farm.

He had a sister and a brother. He started in a country school when he was four years old. When he was 12, he was taken out of school to help his father on the farm.

But he wanted an education. He worked for neighbors and saved his money. He used it for tuition and books. Then he walked three miles to school and back each day. He got a job teaching little children. He kept studying. He wanted to set a good example for the children. One of his students was Zora Della Cooley.

A few years later he joined the church. Zora played the organ and sang in the church. He liked to hear her sing. They fell in love and were married.

They lived with his father and mother on their farm. They had no children. They adopted a niece, Rilla Ethel. Her brother lived with them, too.

Dickinson studied to be a lawyer but didn't pass the bar exam. He used what he learned in politics. He was elected a Michigan Representative three times. He was honest and later he was elected a Michigan Senator.

He went around the state telling people they shouldn't drink liquor. He was called a "Dry." He told them they should let women vote. He told them gambling was bad. He carried his Bible with him and preached sermons. They knew he was a good man. When he ran for an office, they voted for him. He was a Republican.

Dickinson was elected Lieutenant Governor in 1914. It was his job to help the governor. He drove 20 miles to Lansing from Charlotte and back every day. He always wore a proper suit and high laced shoes.

He never did any business on Sundays. He taught Sunday School and went to church. He said legislators should talk less and pray more.

Some politicians poked fun at Dickinson. But the people trusted him. He was elected seven times to be Lieutenant Governor. The last time, Governor Fitzgerald died only 10

weeks after taking office. That made Dickinson the governor. He was 79 years old.

He ordered the State Police to break up all slot machines. Some people signed papers to get him out of office. He said he'd sign the papers, too. "I never wanted to be governor," he said. Everybody laughed and left him alone.

Dickinson named a woman, Matilda Dodge Wilson, to fill his place as Lieutenant Governor. Some politicans worried. He was 80 and if he died, a woman would become governor. But he didn't die. He lost the next election to Murray Van Wagoner. Both Dickinson and Matilda went home.

Zora died about five months before Luren Dickinson left office. He lived on their farm but kept making speeches. He died when he was 84, on April 22, 1943. He was buried beside Zora in the Charlotte cemetery.

GOVERNOR MURRAY D. VAN WAGONER
1941 AND 1942

Pat was a little Dutch boy with an Irish nickname. He was born only a few hours after St. Patrick's Day. His mother and father named him Murray Delos Van Wagoner. But the doctor called him "Pat." The name stuck.

His mother and father were farming near Kingston when Pat was born. (March 18, 1898) He had one brother, Jacob. When Jacob grew up he owned an insurance agency in Pontiac. He had one sister, Esther.

When Esther grew up she wrote for newspapers. She lived in Washington, D.C.

When Pat was three years old they moved to Pontiac. His father sold insurance. Pat and Jacob delivered newspapers for the Pontiac Press. They did odd jobs to earn money.

Pat played in the orchestra in high school. He played football, too. He was a tackle. And he got a girlfriend.

Her name was Helen Jossman. They were sweethearts.

He went to the University of Michigan. Pat played football on the University team until he hurt his knee. He worked nights in a garage to pay his way through Engineering school.

After he graduated he got a job with the State Highway Department. He and Helen were married and had two girls, Ellen Louise and Jo Ann.

Pat liked politics. His mother and father were Republicans. But he ran for an office on the Democratic ticket. He lost. Two years later his friends put his name on a ballot. He won this time. He was the County drain commissioner.

He got to know a lot of people. He liked children, cigars and dogs. He liked to play games like dominoes. He had a big laugh and a big smile. He was a big man too, about 200 pounds.

It was hard for Pat to give talks. Sometimes he would say the wrong things. He took speech lessons to help him.

By 1933, Pat was the State Highway Commissioner and they moved to Lansing. He started building roads all over the state. Everyone knew him. The Democrats got him to run for governor. He won and Governor Dickinson lost.

World War II began soon after Pat took office. He worked hard to see that Michigan had

a defense program. The state began to make things needed in the war.

After two years another governor, Harry Kelly, was elected. Pat wished him well. He made another try for governor in 1946, but this time Kim Sigler beat him.

President Harry Truman appointed Pat to be the Military Governor of Bavaria. The Van Wagoners liked it in Bavaria. It was called the bread basket of Germany. But they came home after two years.

The Van Wagoners lived in Birmingham. Pat had time now to make home movies. He went deer hunting up north. He liked to play golf but wasn't very good at it, he said.

He and Helen had been married for 62 years when she died. He died seven weeks later, on June 12, 1986. He was 88 years old.

GOVERNOR HARRY F. KELLY
1943 THROUGH 1946

Harry Kelly was a World War I hero. He was Governor of Michigan during most of World War II. He always looked out for veterans.

Harry was a twin. He and his twin sister were born on April 19, 1895. They had four younger brothers and three sisters. His father was a lawyer in Ottawa, Illinois. His mother's brother was in the Illinois Legislature. He was Harry's uncle and he liked Harry. They went to political meetings together.

The Kellys had fun. They were a big, happy family.

Harry liked to play baseball. He wanted to grow up to be a lawyer. He graduated from high school. He went to Notre Dame University law school. Then World War I was declared. Harry joined the Army and was an officer. He was sent overseas.

He was wounded in both legs and captured by five Germans. He escaped and was wounded again. He spent a night at the bottom of a trench before he was taken to the medics. He was given their highest medal by the French.

Harry lived but he lost his right leg. He came back home with a wooden leg. He didn't let this stop him. He wanted to be in politics. He was elected an attorney for LaSalle County in Illinois.

Three of his brothers also became lawyers. Their father decided the town was too small for five Kelly lawyers. He moved to Detroit with his son, Emmett. Harry joined them three years later. They were all Republicans.

In Detroit, Harry met Anne O'Brien from the Upper Peninsula. She was a gym teacher. She was a Democrat. Her family was upset when they were married. But Anne and Harry got along fine. They had six children: Joanne, twins Harry, Jr. and Brian, Lawrence, Roger and Mary. Their house was always noisy, like a train depot.

Harry Kelly still wanted to be in politics. He was appointed to some state offices. In 1938 he was elected Secretary of State. He was re-elected for two more years. Then he ran for governor and beat Governor Van Wagoner.

World War II was underway in 1943. Kelly kept on with the war plans for Michigan.

There was a race riot in Detroit. He called out federal troops for help. In 1944, he was re-elected governor. When the war ended he set up a fund to help veterans.

Kelly didn't want to run again for governor. He wanted to be home with his family. He liked to stay at their cabin near Gaylord and swim. His nephew remembered how Kelly would take off his wooden leg and swim "like an otter." He was a big man and liked to wear flannel shirts. He would sit in his wheelchair and tell stories.

But Kelly ran one more time for governor. His friends thought he could beat Governor Williams. He came very close. They had to recount the votes but he lost. Then he ran for the State Supreme Court. He won and was on the Court for 16 years. He liked this work and was very good at it.

Harry Kelly retired from the Court when he was 75 years old. Just six weeks later he died, February 8, 1971. His nephew wrote, "He was an honest man who always gave a honest day's work."

GOVERNOR KIM SIGLER
1947 AND 1948

Kim Sigler was a cowboy. He was a fancy dresser. He loved to fly airplanes.

Kim was born May 2, 1894 on his father's ranch out West in Nebraska. He had a younger sister, Goldie. His mother wanted him to be a doctor or a lawyer. His father wanted him to be a rancher.

When he was seven years old, Kim was riding horses. When he was a teenager, he was roping and branding steers. He did his chores before breakfast.

His father was a veterinarian. They had a home-made boxing ring in their house. Kim liked to box with his father. He was a good boxer. When he was older he boxed for his meals. He had 20 knockouts in 50 fights. In one fight his nose was broken.

In high school Kim played on the football team. He was a catcher on the baseball team. He played a little basketball. He was on the debate team and was a good speaker. He graduated in 1913 and decided to be a lawyer.

Kim came to the University of Michigan. His mother had sewed $40 inside his vest pocket to help him. But he got a job to pay his own way through school.

He liked to canoe on the Huron River. One day a girl fell out of her canoe. She couldn't swim. Kim saved her. Her name was Mae Pierson. She was a studying to be a nurse. They fell in love. When she graduated, they were married.

Kim got a job in the Ford Motor company so he could work at night. In the day he went to law school at the University of Detroit. He graduated in 1918 and was a lawyer. A few years later they moved to Hastings.

They liked Hastings. They had three daughters: Betty, Beverly and Goldie Madalon. Beverly died when she was 11 years old. She had infantile paralysis. They were very sad.

Kim had a beautiful office. People came just to see it. He won many law cases. People came to hear him in court. In 1943 he was asked to be a special prosecutor for the grand jury in Ingham County. His job was to get rid of any crooks in the Michigan Legislature. He and Mae moved to Lansing.

He had a lot of the legislators investigated. Some were found guilty and put in jail. One senator died mysteriously. The senators fired Kim from the job. By this time his name was well-known. He liked to talk to reporters. People liked his fighting spirit.

Kim was a handsome man. He liked to dress in fancy clothes. He had about 50 suits. He wore spats on his shoes. He wore a Western hat. He wore gloves and carried a cane. He wanted to be Governor of Michigan. Mae was sorry she couldn't help him. She was sick and in a wheelchair.

He ran for governor and the people elected him. He cleaned up the prisons. Some of the prisoners had been leaving and coming back when they wanted to. He stopped the hanky-panky. But he made many enemies. Many legislators didn't like him. He'd caused them too much trouble. His own Republican party was not happy with him. He'd caused them trouble, too.

Kim learned to fly an airplane while he was governor. He flew all over and loved it. A lot of voters thought he should be working in his office. He was surprised when they didn't elect him again. He said he was glad they "kicked" him out of office in 1948.

But he stayed in Lansing, in a law office. He kept flying his small plane. He flew to South America and across America to the Arctic circle.

Kim Sigler was lucky until one day in November 1953. His plane crashed near Battle Creek and he was killed. He was 59 years old. He had lived like a shooting star and died in a blaze.

GOVERNOR G. MENNEN WILLIAMS
1949 THROUGH 1960

Gerhard Mennen Williams was called Soapy. His young brothers were called Lather and Suds. This was because their grandfather made Mennen soaps and lotions.

Soapy didn't mind. People called him that all his life.

He was born in Detroit on February 23, 1911. His mother and father were rich. They were very strict and his father paddled the boys when they were naughty. They all went to church on Sundays. Soapy kept a Bible near him all his life. He tried to do his best and then left things up to God.

Soapy's mother and father traveled often and left the children at home with their aunt and uncle. Another uncle took the boys camping and hunting up north. Soapy liked this. He also liked to exercise and took boxing lessons.

He went to grade school in Detroit. He and his brother did odd jobs and saved their 25 cents a week allowances so they could buy bicycles. They wanted bikes to ride to school and save carfare. It was five miles.

When he was 14, Soapy was sent to the Salisbury School in Connecticut. He played football, basketball, baseball and was in track. He got good grades in school. He liked to give speeches, too. One summer he went with Henry and another boy to ride their bicycles through Europe.

Soapy decided he wanted to go into politics so he could help people. Then he went to Princeton University in 1933. He was elected president of the Young Republicans Club. His mother and father were both Republicans.

After he graduated from Princeton he came back home. He studied law at the University of Michigan. He decided he'd like to be Governor of Michigan. He became a Democrat. He met Nancy Quirk of Ypsilanti and after they both graduated, they got married. Then they moved to Washington, D.C. so he could work for the government.

When World War II began, Soapy joined the U.S. Navy. He spent four years in the Pacific doing intelligence work. He earned 10 battle stars and two medals. He was a lieutenant commander when he came home.

He began to work for the government in Detroit. Governor Kim Sigler appointed him to a Commission. Soapy met a lot of people in this job and decided to run for governor in 1948. First he had to get the Democratic party back together. Friends helped him.

Soapy's mother wouldn't give money to Democrats. So he and Nancy borrowed cash on their house from the bank. They drove an old car all over Michigan to get people to vote for him. They had to leave their three children home: Gerhard Mennen, Jr., Nancy Quirk and Wendy.

People liked Soapy. He was very tall, good-looking, good-natured and kind. Some did not agree with what he said, but they liked him and they voted for him. Labor unions and Democrats worked together for him. He won the election and became governor.

Work on the Mackinac Bridge was completed while he was governor. He did not get all the things to help people that he wanted. But he was stubborn and got some important laws passed. He was re-elected

five times and was governor for 12 years. This set a record and he did not run again in 1960.

Soapy was soon appointed to go to Africa by President John Kennedy. He spent five years making friends there for the United States. Then he was named U.S. Ambassador to the Philippines for a year.

In 1970 Soapy Williams was elected to the State Supreme Court for eight years. He was re-elected for another eight years and retired in 1986.

Two years later he died at the age of 76. He was buried in the cemetery on Mackinac Island. It was a military funeral which he would have liked.

GOVERNOR JOHN B. SWAINSON
1961 AND 1962

John Swainson was born in Canada, July 31, 1925. His mother and father brought him to Port Huron when he was a little baby. He had one brother and one sister.

Everyone liked John. He was friendly and had a happy smile. He was a Boy Scout and became an Eagle Scout. In high school he was captain of his football team.

When John graduated from high school, he joined the Army in World War II. He was with General Patton's troops in France. One night a land mine exploded and blew up his jeep. His leg was blown off below the knee. His other leg was also hurt so bad it had to be amputated. He woke up in a hospital. He was glad to be alive.

John was given many medals for bravery. He was sent back to the United States. He learned to walk again at Percy Jones Hospital in Battle Creek. Then he decided to go to Olivet College. It is near Battle Creek.

At Olivet College, John met pretty Alice Nielsen and they were married. He hurt his leg again when he was tobogganing. They had to move south where there was no snow. They moved to North Carolina.

John kept on going to school. He graduated from law school at the University of North Carolina. Then they moved back to Detroit. Next they moved to Plymouth and he ran for the Michigan Senate. He won the election in 1954 and was re-elected two years later. He took the train back and forth to Lansing.

The Swainsons built a house. They had three children: John, Hans and Kristina. Then John was elected Lieutenant Governor to work with Governor Mennen Williams.

When Williams didn't run again for governor, John Swainson did. He was 35 years old when he was elected. The family moved to Lansing. They lived there for two years. Then George Romney, a Republican, won the next election.

Swainson practiced law in Detroit until he was elected a Circuit Court Judge in Wayne County. Five years later he was elected to the State Supreme Court.

By now the Swainsons had bought a large farm near Manchester. They called it the Hustings. For five years he was on the Supreme Court. Then he was accused of accepting a bribe. He was found "not guilty." But he was charged with not telling the truth to the grand jury. He resigned from the Court and he lost his license to practice law.

It was the worst time of his life. He felt all alone and didn't want to face people. But his family and true friends stood beside him. He became an antique dealer and discovered a love for history. He got back his license to practice law. In 1985 he was appointed to the Michigan Historical Commission. He became president of the commission.

GOVERNOR GEORGE W. ROMNEY
1963 TO JANUARY 22, 1969

George Romney worked hard all his life. When he was seven years old his job was to hoe potatoes on the family farm in Utah. When he was 11 years old he worked in sugar beet fields for farmers. He earned $1 an acre for thinning the beets.

That was just the beginning. He's never stopped working.

George was born on July 8, 1907 in Mexico. His father had moved there from the United States with other Mormon families. When George was five years old the Mexicans started fighting the Americans. The Romneys had to escape to Texas. Later they moved to Salt Lake City, Utah.

George had three older brothers, two younger brothers and a sister. His father was a carpenter and built houses. They were poor but they were a happy family. They helped each other and they prayed together.

When George was in high school he went out for football. He was so small that no uniform would fit him. He had to tie up his pant legs and sleeves with shoelaces. But he didn't give up. He grew larger and got to be a team player. He also played basketball and baseball. When he was a senior he earned letters in all three sports.

While he was in high school George met Lenore LaFount. He fell in love with her and years later they were married. They had four children: Lynn, Jane, Scott and Mitt.

George spent a year as a missionary for the Mormon Church in the British Isles. He learned to talk to people. This was good training, he said. When he returned to the United States he went to the University of Utah. Lenore was at the University in Washington, D.C., so George went there too. He got a job working for a senator.

George and Lenore were married in 1931. They lived in Washington for eight years. Then he got a job in Detroit and they moved there. A few years later (1954) he became president of American Motors Corporation. He said the big automobile companies were making dinosaurs. They were losing money. His company made small Ramblers. In four years they began to make a profit. He told people what to do and they did it.

When the state ran out of money, he decided Michigan needed a new constitu-

tion. He went to Lansing and helped write one. Then he ran for governor and was elected in 1962. Now when he told people what to do, they didn't always do it. But he got a lot done and he was re-elected. Two years later the new constitution was law and he was re-elected for four years.

In 1967, George Romney got the legislature to pass an income tax. The state had enough money now to pay for things it needed. But then there were riots in Detroit. It was a bad time for everyone. There were seven days of terror and 40 people died. There were fires and blocks of buildings burned down. Romney called federal troops to put things in order.

That fall, Romney decided to run for President of the United States. Months later he changed his mind and Richard Nixon was nominated and elected. President Nixon named Romney to his Cabinet and he went to Washington, D.C. in 1969.

The Romneys lived in a hotel in Washington. They let him jog mornings on the roof. They also let him pick a rose each morning for Lenore. When he resigned in 1973, the Romneys came back to their home in Bloomfield Hills. Today he is 86 years old. He is working to get people in Michigan to volunteer to help each other. He believes people do not need government to do the things they can do for themselves.

GOVERNOR WILLIAM G. MILLIKEN
1969 THROUGH 1982

Bill Milliken was born and raised up north in Traverse City. He left for school. He left for the war. He left for Lansing to be in the government. But he always came back to this beautiful country with the clean, clear air.

His grandfather and his father were both Michigan Senators. They were both good businessmen, too. They owned the Milliken Department store.

Bill was born on March 26, 1922. He had an older brother, John, who grew up to be a doctor. He had a younger sister, Ruth. His mother and father were strict and the children had their chores to do.

On Sunday afternoons young Bill liked to go to nearby Interlochen. His mother took him to concerts there. He enjoyed music and art.

Bill liked animals. He had a German Shepherd dog named Eric. He loved to ride a horse, King High. He liked school, too, and was a good student. In high school he played in the band. He wrote for the school paper. He played tennis and basketball. His basketball team won a State Championship in 1940.

Bill also liked government. He was president of his freshman class and school governor when he was a senior. He went with his father to political meetings. He listened to his father talk. In his heart he wanted to be in government, too. Maybe governor someday? But there was much to do first.

On Saturdays he swept floors in his father's store. In summers he worked in a gas station. He saved his money and bought a car with his brother. It had six horns on it run by three buttons. It also had a flat tire on the way home after they bought it.

Then he went to Yale University in Connecticut for three years. But World War II was going on and he joined the U.S. Army Air Force. He became a waist gunner on a B-24 bomber. He lived through two crashes and bailed out once over Italy. He was wounded by flak on one flight. He was given many medals for his bravery.

After he returned from the war, Bill married Helen Wallbank from Denver. He finished his last year at Yale. They came back to Traverse City and they had two children, William Jr., and Elaine. He ran the Milliken Department store and made it grow.

In 1960, William Milliken ran for Michigan Senator on the Republican ticket. He won the election and was a senator in Lansing until 1964. Then he was elected Lieutenant Governor. He helped Governor Romney. They won more elections.

When Governor Romney left for a new job in Washington, D.C., in 1969, Milliken took his place.

Now Milliken could do some things he wanted to do for Michigan. He worked to improve the environment in the state. He wanted to protect the Great Lakes. He tried to get special help for Detroit.

Many Democrats and some Republicans did not agree with Milliken. But he worked with them. If he got angry, it only showed in his eyes. Some politicians called him a "good guy" governor. He always stood firm for his beliefs. "You should do what you believe is right," he said. And he always told the truth.

The people liked him and trusted him. They voted for him again and again. He was Governor for 14 years. This is the longest time any man has been Governor of Michgian.

Governor Milliken decided in 1982 to go back to his home in Traverse City. He is happy there and still doing many good things for Michigan.

GOVERNOR JAMES J. BLANCHARD
1983 THROUGH 1990

His uncle said that some day Jamie Blanchard would be Governor of Michigan.

But Jamie wanted to be a baseball player when he grew up. He rode his bike by the Detroit Tigers Stadium. He wanted to see Al Kaline. He collected baseball cards.

Jamie was born on August 8, 1942, and lived in Ferndale, Michigan. He had one sister, Suzanne, who was four years older than he was. When Jamie was nine years old, he and Suzanne went with their mother to visit their grandmother. When they came back home, their father had gone away. They did not see him again for a long time.

His mother worked in an office. Jamie liked to go to a Democratic party headquarters near their house. He had a big smile and everyone liked him. When he was 10 years old they paid him 50 cents an hour to help them. He decided to be a politican. He wanted to be a congressman and go to Washington.

In high school, Jamie was elected president of his freshman class. When he was a senior he was president of the Student Council. He got a letter in track, but he liked politics best.

He went to Michigan State University. He was elected president of his classes two times. Then he went to law school at the University of Minnesota.

When he had his law degree, Jamie came back to Michigan. He worked in a law office in Lansing. Now he was married and had a little boy, Jay. But he still wanted to go to Washington.

His friends helped him and he was elected to Congress four times. He spent eight years in Washington. Then, Jamie decided to come back to Michigan. He ran for governor. The Democrats had been fighting with the unions, but they made up. They all worked to get Jamie elected governor.

He won the election. His uncle had been right. Jamie was Governor of Michigan for eight years. When he ran for a third time, he lost to John Engler.

James Blanchard got a job in Washington and he helped William J. Clinton become President. Then President Clinton named him U.S. Ambassador to Canada in 1993.

GOVERNOR JOHN ENGLER
1991-

John Engler was the oldest child in the family. He was raised on his parents' 600-acre farm with his two brothers and four sisters. He was born on October 12, 1948. Their big farm was near Mt. Pleasant, Michigan. They raised beef cattle; Herefords, Angus and Charolais.

When John was 10 years old he joined a 4H Club. He took his steers to show at the Isabella County Fair. He won so many ribbons that they filled a big box.

He also showed his steers at the Michigan State Fair. But he never had a Grand Champion steer.

He helped his brothers and sisters when they were old enough to show their steers at the fairs. Then they won five Grand Champion ribbons. When he was older, he was in Future Farmers of America (FFA).

John had to get up early and work hard many days on the farm. He helped plant corn and cut it for silage to feed the beef cattle. He helped put hay in bales and haul it to the barn on a wagon behind a tractor. There was always lots to do and there wasn't much time for fun.

In school, John was a good student. He liked to read. He even read the newspaper before the school bus came in the mornings. He liked to read about government and politics. In high school he played football. His team didn't win any games, but he played as hard as he could and didn't give up.

After he graduated from high school, John went to Michigan State University. He got a job in the beef barn to pay his way. When he was a junior, he was elected president of his dormitory.

By the time John graduated from college he wanted to be a State Representative in Lansing. He drew up a plan to win the election. He met people and talked to them. They trusted him. They voted for him and he won the election. He was only 22 years old.

After that John won many elections. He beat three men who had been in office a long time. They began to call him "John the Giant Killer". He became a Michigan Senator. While he was a senator he went to law school and graduated. Then he wanted to make changes in the government.

He wanted to lower taxes so people wouldn't lose their homes. He wanted to make the government smaller, not larger.

To help people who truly cannot help themselves. He decided he'd have to be the governor to do this. So he drew up a new plan and worked harder than ever. He won the election.

A month before he took office he married a girl from Texas. Everyone was surprised. Her name is Michelle and she is a lawyer, too.

Today he is Governor John Engler. And he is making changes.